About the Author

Austin Gardner is a student at University of Findlay, Ohio. He holds an undergraduate degree in Sport and Event Management and is working toward his Master of Arts in Education: Human Resource Development with a Leadership Emphasis. He is from Bowling Green, Ohio, where he attended a private Jesuit high school in Toledo (St. John's Jesuit). He is a member of the UF basketball team (twice named team captain), is Vice President of the Fellowship of Christian Athletes (voted FCA Leader of the Year in the 2016–2017 school year), is the President of the Student Athlete Advisory Committee, is an orientation leader, and he volunteers his time at the Hancock County Special Olympics. His future goals are to become a collegiate basketball coach and to continue to help others grow in their faith while guiding them to achieve their goals.

I wrote this book because I found myself reading many books about coaches, athletes, and religion. Those books helped me in my faith, lifestyle, and mindset. I wanted to write this book, so I could give back to other people in which it can help them grow in their faith and journey through life.

I was inspired to write this book because of my ups and downs of injuries. God was my inspiration. He has put me in tough situations mentally, physically, emotionally, and spiritually. I have leaned on the Lord for my strength and wisdom.

I have used scripture readings from the Holy NIV translation of the Bible and communicated my experiences through the different encounters I have had from training camps, organizations, and conversations I have had with other individuals.

Introduction

Life can hit you in so many ways. It can hit you mentally, physically, and figuratively. No one likes to be hit, but sometimes being hit makes you stronger. If you get hit only one time, it hurts badly, and if you get hit again, you think, why me? If you get hit a third time, most people think the world is out to get them. This is the perspective of a negative person. Why not look at it another way? The first time you get hit, why not say, "That felt good, I cannot wait for the next hit." Bam! Another hit comes and now you are prepared to get hit with all the punches that life throws at you. Accept the hits and turn it into motivation.

There are many ways to help with the rollercoaster that life brings. I have handled adversity many ways, mainly dealing with athletics and the injuries that go along with playing a sport.

My injuries have included:

1. A broken left tibia in preschool while roller blading and playing basketball.
2. A broken left ankle while playing basketball in both the fifth and sixth grades.
3. A broken left foot in sixth grade.
4. A broken left wrist in eleventh grade.

5. Torn ankle ligaments in the twelfth grade.
6. Patellar tendon surgery on left knee in Redshirt Freshman.
7. Patellar tendon surgery on left knee in Redshirt Junior.

Do you believe that everything happens for a reason? Whether or not you do, it does not matter. I believe that things happen in life because God is bringing out more in you than you believe in yourself. He is diving deeper into your mind, heart, and soul, trying to find out how you will react, and to make you a tougher individual. God is the greatest above all, and His guidance is the key to putting everything in perspective. I have struggled with injuries, but many other people have had it worse. I think about how great I truly have it, even when I am injured. God has a plan, and I am here to follow it.

Injuries have brought me closer to God in my relationship with Him. Why are you not following God? What is blocking you from having a deep relationship with God? Is it time? Do you not care enough?

Do you think you do not need Him? Or is life too good right now and you are not facing any challenges? What if you are hit with a challenge such as an injury? Who do you lean on now? Is it your own strength? Someone else's? Or is it Jesus's, the one who died on the cross for our sins? The one who is always there for us during our good and bad times.

What is your story?

My Story

My name is Austin Gardner, and I am from Bowling Green, Ohio. I was raised by my parents, Randy and Sandy. I have two siblings, Brooks and Christina. I grew up like any youngest child who has a big brother: I tried to be like him. I competed against him in everything from sports to video games. If I wanted to do something less competitive, then I had my sister with whom to hang out. I had a well-balanced life with parents who were protective and caring and siblings who helped me grow and learn from their mistakes.

I was not the smartest kid in school. I took speech class and other comprehensive reading courses because I struggled in those areas. I was very blessed with my athletic ability; however, I grew up playing nearly every sport. At one time or another, I played soccer, baseball, roller hockey, basketball, golf, football, and ran cross country. I only focused on two sports in high school though: golf and basketball.

I began playing golf in the eighth grade. Many family members on my dad's side played the sport. I had a very successful golfing career considering that I did not play for very long. I played on the varsity team during my freshman, sophomore, and junior years of high school. Basketball was my favorite sport; however, golf helped me learn many things including patience, emotional balance, and appreciation of the outdoors. I got to cherish the nature that God created. I played in the rain, wind, cold, heat, and sometimes even snow flurries. It made me tough mentally. One cannot physically do anything special in golf, but a golf shot can be played many ways.

I had to know when to risk trying to hit a green in regulation on a par-5 hole or to just lay up short of the green to play it safe. Golf is like life; the game is eighteen holes and takes around five hours to play. A game cannot be saved in one shot or one hole, but several consistent shots can get the game back on track. Life is the same way. Life is a long journey; one decision may not make or break it, but it can have an impact on it. Making all the right little decisions will add up and change one's life drastically.

I decided not to play golf in my senior year, and I do not regret my decision because I was doing what was best for me and helping myself grow as a person.

Basketball is a sport that I have played my whole life. I have always continued to play, no matter what. I played on my brother's team when I was in first grade. It did not matter what age the other players were because I thought I belonged on the team because I believed I was good enough. Whenever I had the opportunity to play, I gave it my best and made the most of it. I was always the best player on my school teams, and even on some of my Amateur Athletic Union (AAU) teams. I started AAU in the fourth grade, which gave me many chances to travel and play basketball. Exposure did not matter at that grade level, but I played anyway. I enjoyed playing basketball, but no one was going to recruit me at that age.

I had a tough decision to make about where I wanted to go to high school. This decision was difficult for me because I was going to leave my hometown, friends, and the school system I am comfortable with. My options were to stay in the Bowling Green School District or to find a school in Toledo.

For my eighth grade year, I decided to try out Toledo's St. John's Jesuit High School and Academy. I knew some of the students there because of playing basketball. It was different from Bowling Green because it was a Catholic, college-prep, boys' school where I had to wear a shirt and tie every day. The school was not for everyone, but it was for me. I was extremely happy with my decision.

As a student with the goal of playing collegiate basketball, I unfortunately did not make the junior varsity team as a freshman. But I took my role as the freshman point guard to heart, and I helped guide the freshman team to the first perfect season of 20–0. It was a fun season with a bunch of great teammates. Academics were very difficult for me at St. John's my freshmen year; however, I maintained around a 2.8 grade point average. The following season I jumped from playing on the freshman team to playing varsity basketball. I got to play my first varsity game against Shaker Heights, a team that had a former University of Louisville and current Celtics player Terry Rozier. Rozier was a senior when I was a junior in high school at Toledo St. John's. I grew a lot that year, and I played my role as a backup point guard well.

We finished the season 20–3, as we lost in the district championship game to a team we had beaten earlier in the season by twenty-three points. I continued to work hard academically because some of the English, math, and science classes were a challenge for me. My grades were improving, but not by much.

My junior season came around and time was flying by. I became the starting point guard and had a teammate named Marc Loving who had already committed to play for Ohio State. We had high expectations like every other year, and we wanted to make our run to the State Final Four. Our season was going well until I got undercut in a game against Detroit Jesuit and fell on my wrist. The accident happened on the first play of the second half. I did not think anything of it, and I continued to grind in a close game even through my wrist cracked while running up and down the court. We won by three points that game; it was a great team win. I walked into school the next day, and I told my coach that my wrist was still hurting badly. I could not move it. I went to the hospital to get it checked, and it was a clean break. I was going to miss five to six weeks of basketball because of the injury.

I came back a week early to try and finish the season on a positive note. Unfortunately, we lost the district game by three points to one of my future Findlay teammates and college roommate, Ricardo Smith, and Wisconsin basketball star, Nigel Hayes. We finished the season 15–7.

I had a rough junior season because of injuries, and I did not have a great golfing season. I was still just getting by academically and needed to make some changes moving forward into my senior year at St. John's.

Senior year is supposed to be special and memorable. I wanted to win a state championship in basketball more than anything. I did not play golf my senior season due to college visits, recruiting, and focusing on my senior season of basketball. Golf was frustrating, and I was not enjoying it as much as I would have hoped.

I committed to the University of Findlay on October 11, 2012, and signed on November 14 to continue my academic and basketball career. I had been considering Findlay and several other Division II and Division I schools who had been recruiting me.

Findlay was ideal because of the location and the championships they have won. I thought it was the best decision for my family and me.

My senior season was going as planned; we were winning many games, we went out to Arizona to play some games, and I continued to grow as a man. We were 20–3 heading into our district game against Toledo Rogers. We beat them earlier in the season, and we were ranked number one in the state.

Everything changed the night before the game. I had a number of ankle injuries the previous summers, and in the last ten minutes of practice, I stepped on a teammate's foot and tore three ligaments in my ankle. I worked hard the next day to ensure that I could still play. I started therapy in the morning, skipped class to ice, and shot baskets in the gym the rest of the day.

I warmed up for the game while trying to fight through the pain. I had a steroid battery connected to my ankle, six taped rods, a taped ankle, and an ankle brace. I tried my hardest to play and try to make the dream of winning the championship happen. I told my coach, Ed Heintschel, ten minutes before the game that I could not go on. A tear ran down his face as he hugged me.

I could run with a limp but could not cut or move side to side. We lost that night 66–55, and I felt as if my career at St. John's was a failure. I felt like I let the team down, the school down, my family and myself down. I was heartbroken. I was graduating in seven weeks, and I knew there was something missing.

Attending a Kairos retreat changed my perspective and outlook on my experience at St. John's. I realized I was going to graduate from one of the best schools in Ohio, I was going to continue my academic and athletic career for free thanks to a scholarship, I was growing into a man, and I was growing spiritually. Kairos put these things in perspective because of all the letters I received from friends and family and the lives I had touched outside of basketball. I grew with the St. John's motto of "being a man for others." I got to speak at the president's dinner. This president's dinner was for alums to donate back to the school. I was chosen because of the tough experience I went through athletically, but I got more than just athletics out of my experience. I got to speak about all of my experiences, and that was easy to talk about because I spoke from the heart. God gave me the vision to see outside of my dream by looking at the big picture.

I made an impact on so many students, faculty members, teammates, and family members who I did not even think about because my dream was too narrow. Yes, I wish we would have won that state championship, but would I have then seen the vision God gave me, which was more important than winning a championship?

During my freshman year of college, I practiced some of the same qualities I had always portrayed such as caring, giving, and helping others, but I did not keep my faith the way I should have. I got caught up in the college life of just being independent and on my own. I went to parties just to hang out with my team, but I never drank alcohol. I wanted to fit in even though the scenery was not for me. I went through the motions my freshmen year and played the role of backup point guard. It was tough to go from being a high school star back to a regular player. But I adapted to it and accepted it because I was part of a team. We had a great season, and I got to contribute to a championship team that made it to the National Collegiate Athletic Association (NCAA) Tournament.

I battled through a knee injury all year that year and went through rehabilitation all summer and fall. Nevertheless, I had to have knee surgery, which was not guaranteed to fix my problem. The surgery did not work, and I went through rehab all over again, seeing physical therapists, doctors, trainers, and strength coaches. No one really understood my knee injury and the season was approaching again very soon.

I tried to play and suck it up, but it was so painful. I had to grind through it. I was not playing much, and I felt pointless, useless, and lost. I had to decide whether to accept my role or to do something about it. I committed myself to Christ. I was a believer in Him, and it was time for me to do something about it. I decided not to face life alone, but to go with Him. He guided me with the right mindset and put me back on the path I needed to live the life I wanted. I became a better team player, my knee got healthier, I got more involved in campus organizations, and I became a starter on the team. After a 2–4 start, we finished the season 20–8. I was proud of the way we competed. My knee was doing poorly again; however, I had a stem cell procedure following the season.

I was in rehabilitation again all summer just to get myself ready to play again for my medical redshirt junior season. The season started at Dayton, and we had them down early in the game 26–10. They came back at us repeatedly and defeated us 76–69 in front of the sold-out University of Dayton Arena. We were officially ready for our home opener.

The season progressed, and my knee got worse and worse. The final game of my redshirt junior season was at Ferris State. The game was tied 76–76 with about twenty-nine seconds to go. I went to the basket and got fouled. When I went into my shooting motion, I felt my knee give out. I could jump off the ground, but I went down in immense pain. Ricardo Smith made one free throw and that was the winning point for us. We moved to 4–2 with momentum moving forward. I did not practice for the next two days, but the day before the next game I thought I should get some reps in. I was jogging after the ball, already in a lot of pain, and my knee gave out. I went down on the floor knowing that that was it. I needed to see a doctor. I met with several doctors, all who thought that my college career was over. This is not how I wanted to go out, but I accepted God's plan for me.

After not playing well at Ferris State in the Great Lakes Intercollegiate Athletic Conference (GLIAC) Tournament and losing by thirty-one points, we had switched the script by being the sixth seed in the NCAA Division II Tournament. We beat Southern Indiana 70–69 in a hard-fought game on both ends of the floor. Sure enough, we played our league champion Ferris State in the Round of 32. We defeated Ferris State 68–63. Our intensity and focus were on a whole new level, and if we would had played that way every game that season we would have been even better. We then had the opportunity to take on Bellarmine University, the number one seed in the region and the host school for the Sweet Sixteen. I was so excited to see my teammates succeed even though I would have liked to have played on a big stage with them. This is an example of not taking special moments for granted. Watching my teammates succeed was one of the best feelings I have had because I was able to reflect on the special careers with the ones I started my collegiate career.

I officially graduated from the University of Findlay in May 2017. I had one of the best commencement speakers I could ask for, and that was my dad. There was only one criteria he had to follow if he was going to speak at my graduation: he could only mention me one time in his speech. If he mentioned me more than once then he would have to mention everyone else who was graduating that day because it was not just my day; the day belonged to all the students from UF who were graduating. I was excited and blessed to graduate from such a great institution.

After graduation, I realized my journey was not over yet at Findlay. I was starting my Master's in Arts of Education: Human Resource Development in the summer of 2017, and my goal was to complete it by summer of 2018. I had an extremely busy summer with rehabilitation, classes, mini-vacations, and Ultimate Training Camp in Boston which shaped my vision on God, sports, and life. I was fully committed to finishing my five years at Findlay. My last year would be the best one yet, not just for myself, but for the other people I encounter every day by touching them with faith, love, and motivation.

My fifth and final year at the University of Findlay was going to be one that was not very predictable: starting my graduate studies, not knowing if I would be able to fully compete in college athletics again, continuing to pursue all my efforts in the organizations I am involved in, and trying to find a job in 2018. There were so many question marks. There were many turns my last year at Findlay could go take, but I had no concerns. I was grounded in my faith that no matter what would happen, I would be in good hands with God. He had brought me to this day, and He will continue to guide me down His path.

All in One

Life is a lot to handle sometimes but breaking it down into three life-changing words will help you as person as well as the world. There are many ways to go about changing your life, but what is the right way? What way do you go about living your life? Is it working for you? If it is working for you now, will this way also work in the future? I have been working on a new version of myself recently. I have found myself getting comfortable by first getting uncomfortable. It is difficult to change something you have been accustomed to doing for a long time. So, how do you get out of that routine? Why do people want to start a new program, whether it is a diet plan, an exercise routine, or maybe attending church more often? Whatever that change is, where does it need to start?

If you believe you can make a change in your life and are willing to try, you can do it. It does not start with changing your diet, it does not start by exercising more, and it does not start by going to church more often. Yes, those things are great changes and are all good things to do, but they will be hard to sustain without help. If you have faith, then change can happen.

God is the best trainer, coach, teacher, and motivator. It does not matter if you make mistakes in the things you are trying to change; He will train and teach you the right way. If you make a mistake, He will still love you. And if you want to give up on changing yourself, He will motivate you and keep you moving forward.

Faith is the starting point in making a significant change in your life. If you believe in Him, but do not have a relationship with God, then you still need to instill faith in Him and in yourself. Just because faith is the number one thing you need to change yourself for the better, it does not mean you can love Him one day and then not love Him because something did not go your way. Continue to trust in His plan. Jeremiah 29:11 states, "For I know the plans I have for you, declares the Lord, plans to prosper you and not to harm you, plans to give you hope and a future." God has never given up on us, so why should we give up on His plan for us? He knows the greatest plan for us, so trust and believe in the plan by believing in Him.

The first step is the most difficult one because walking in your faith will be the hardest challenge in your life.

Faith is incorporated in everything you do. If you want to make a positive change for a better version of yourself and others, then make that change. The next change after you have faith and lay down your life for God is learning how to love. It is a simple word, but we all have different definitions of love because there are so many meanings and interpretations of it. Leviticus 19:18 says, "Do not seek revenge or bear a grudge against one of your people but love your neighbor as yourself." We all want to be treated with respect, so why not treat others with respect? Respect is love.

    Having faith is believing in what scripture offers. God says to love others. This commandment includes being loving even when you are unhappy with yourself; do not take your unhappiness out on anyone. If everyone in the world loved each other, think about how peaceful the world would be. It is crazy to think about, but it is true. Whatever you are doing in life, make sure you love what you do. If you are doing chores around the house, doing homework, or performing a task at your job, love what you do. This advice seems very basic, but some people dread going to work or doing chores. Yes, it may not seem like fun at first, but just try going in with a positive mindset.

This suggestion may also seem crazy, but if you love doing everything you do then there is no bad part of the day. You are worshiping God by loving others, loving yourself, and, most importantly, loving Him.

The last change you need to make is motivating others. If you are faithful and are willing to dive into the Word, trust God's promise, and love those around you and everything you do, then why not motivate someone else to do the same? God has given us all talents and abilities to make a difference in the world, but sometimes we distance ourselves from God and never know what our purpose is in life. However, with faith and love you can change more lives than you can imagine. God's children are on Earth right now, so why not help someone who needs to be found? Help them find themselves by finding their relationship with God the Father and His son, Jesus. Help disciple others by helping them discover themselves in the Lord is something that is the greatest gift that a motivator can give. It is time to build the foundation of faith, love, and motivation.

Faith

How to Come to God

Finding yourself in a relationship with God can be a very complicated, even more so than dating, marriage, or friendship. But it doesn't have to be. You may not know where to start or where to go in your relationship with Him. Do not think too much about it. Walk to God by being yourself. He knows who you are now and who He wants you to be. God knows where you are in your life and knows your daily thought processes. Ask God to show you your heart and ask Him to search your heart in a way that can help build your relationship with Him. He knows what is best for you, and by pouring out your heart to Him, you will feel accepted. God has a reason for your existence; therefore, we must lay down our life to Him if we want to see changes in our lives. Deuteronomy 31:6 says, "Be strong and courageous. Do not be afraid or terrified because of them, for the Lord your God goes with you; he will never leave you nor forsake you." Accepting God in your life means giving your life to Him in a way that is strong and courageous.

Someone having courage means that they will not have pain or danger because they are brave.

God shields us and protects us from harm. He protects our minds, heart, and soul. Not everyone can do this, but when you tell the Lord daily in prayer and through your acts throughout the day that you are willing to give your life to Him, then the second part of this Bible verse will be true to you. "He will never leave you nor forsake you" because God goes with you. When you are in your darkest times with no one around you, God is with you and is comforting you through the good and the bad. There is no need to be afraid because the Lord has set a place for us in eternal life, which is the greatest place to be after life on earth.

Romans 15:13 says, "May the God of hope fill you with all joy and peace as you trust in him, so that you may overflow with hope by the power of the Holy Spirit." God fills us with joy and peace even when we do not trust in Him. However, we will feel the gracious power of the Holy Spirit pouring down on us when we trust in the Lord. Trusting someone is hard to do if you do not know that person well. When you want to know God, or you already trust in God, you will feel more accepting of yourself, other family and friends, and, most importantly, your trust in God will expand.

We all know one person who is untrustworthy, but most of us also have one person we can fully trust. That person is willing to listen and to challenge us to make us better, and we are able to talk to them in our lowest points of the day. You can fully trust God in the same way that you trust your best friend but on a whole new level. He is all-knowing and all-loving.

We are not always able to be our true selves at every part of the day. This may be because of being at different events and settings, meeting someone new, being around friends, or communicating with upper-level management at work. We are not likely to act the same way we do around our friends as we would a CEO. That is just the nature of the world. Our relationship with God makes us be ourselves no matter what the setting is or who we talk to because God is with us, and no matter what happens throughout the day, we can always be our true selves. This is the power of faith.

What's Holding You Back?

What is holding you back from where you want to go in life? What is taking you away from the path to be the best person you can be? If there are obstacles in your way, do not avoid them . . . attack them! Most people try to avoid life's obstacles, whether they be their own weaknesses or previous mistakes they've made. But facing these obstacles is a great way to learn and grow. The song "Who Am I" by Casting Crowns is a very emotional and expressional song. It tells us that the Lord has set us up for the greatest strength we have. These lyrics show us that we do not have any weaknesses; we only have those areas in which we need to improve and work harder.

Personally, I was held back from outsiders and always tried to please everyone. But it is not possible to please everyone. We all can be held back from outsiders such as parents, other relatives, friends, or coaches. We need to stay true to ourselves on who we are and who God is intending us to be. Caleb Williams, my former graduate assistant basketball coach at the University of Findlay said, "You cannot always say yes; sometimes no is the best answer." It is hard for me to say no to someone, especially when I can help someone with something.

I need to continue to work on saying no, and I will get better with practice.

I was held back by outsiders; however, I quit looking at how others might look at me. "Oh, he may not be much fun because he doesn't drink; he cares way too much about basketball; he is well known by people on campus and is very involved, which makes him a nerd." Whatever those critics may have said, I can walk away from my college experience saying that I did everything for other people and improved myself as a human being along the way. The second half of my collegiate time at Findlay, I followed God's plan for me, not "Austin's plan." I got active in athletics, my faith, events and organizations on campus, and became more involved in the community. Participating in these activities was my calling, and now nothing has held me back because God helped me find myself.

You might already know what is holding you back, but you are still trying to be cool. There is nothing wrong with that, but you do not want to go back and say, "I wish I changed my college experience by going out more or not going out as much."

If you go through college the way God wants you to, then you will not have to think ten years down the road that another way could have been better. It is never too late to start a new path that is best for you. You can do it as a freshman, sophomore, junior, senior, graduate student, or even after college, but do not say you were held back by someone or something that could have helped you push yourself to be the best you can be. There are so many resources, organizations, students, and faculty members on a college campus to help you succeed in whatever you want out of life.

By believing in God, He will lift you up from the ground and bring you under His wings. He is there for us when we are unaware of His love. He provides us with the strength to grow and to block out the bad while bringing the good into our lives.

God Is Not Far, but Sometimes He Is Hard to Reach

I grew up in a family that attended church regularly. I attended Bethlehem Church in Pemberville, Ohio, where I was baptized. I was confirmed in April 2008 at St. Mark's Lutheran Church in Bowling Green, Ohio. I stopped attending church as often once junior high and high school began, and it affected my life. Church was a great place for quiet time, peace, and reflection, but I got very consumed with AAU basketball because of the demanding schedule to be recruited.

I attended a Catholic high school and just went through the motions of spiritually at first. The main reason I just went through the motions was because I was distracted by all my friends in Mass. I eventually matured and truly tried to find myself and grow in my faith. This newfound awareness led me to attend youth group. I enjoyed the atmosphere of being with my friends who were there because of their faith and not because they were required to be. I tried to go every Wednesday night because it was exactly what I needed to get me to my stable place outside of athletics. I began to fall back into God's hands.

Attending the Kairos retreat during my senior year of high school hit me hard because everyone broke out of their shell. I have kept all my letters that were written to me by many of my loved ones that night. I became emotional and reflected on what my parents, my friend Nick Felhaber, Mr. Harms (my sophomore English teacher), and other classmates I did not associate with much all said about me.

One of the most memorable letters I received was from a former golf teammate and friend. He was in the same graduating class as I. We knew each other but did not communicate often. He is very intelligent and went on to Harvard for college. He wrote a letter to me in which he described how I gave him the best experience of his high school career because I had decided not to play golf my senior year. My absence opened another spot on the varsity team, on which he had never played in his first three years. Everyone saw him as an academic standout, a guy who helped in the community, and a pretty good athlete. By me not playing, this classmate of mine got to play varsity golf on a great team. I had not played for selfish reasons. His letter opened my eyes. I had made a positive and memorable impact on someone's high school career, something I did not realize at the time. This proved to me that there is a big God.

I grew closer to my faith once again because of this experience, and I had an awesome senior year at St. John's Jesuit.

I lost almost all my faith when I went to college. After all the great strides I had made, I began to lose what I had built. It was easy to get caught up in basketball, friends, dorm life, and being independent. I did not bring my faith with me. My freshman year I had zero faith in the sense of going to church and praying every day, which made life difficult at times. My sophomore year I had knee surgery and questioned, why me? It was a hit I took in life, but I realized I would be back out on the court the next year and would be just fine. But the surgery did not work, and the season was approaching quickly. I was not going to be a starter or be in the position I thought I would be in. I was miserable during the first couple of games because of lack of playing time, and I was frustrated about having an unhealthy knee. While all these things were awful, I had two people to comfort me: my mom and dad. They were great to talk to, but they did not live on campus with me. Who was someone I could lean on? I found myself praying and talking to God more. I persevered with Him, which motivated me and brought fire to my everyday life.

Praying and communicating with God moved me to another level. I stopped thinking about excuses, and instead started thinking about how great my life is and how blessed I am. My attitude translated on the court.

No one knew the pain I was going through with my knee, and I played so hard against Lake Superior State when we got embarrassed up there. I realized that our team needed a different identity, and I wanted to be the change we needed. God helped me find my identity, and it was time for me to give our team its identity. Our team practice the Friday before our game at Northwood was brutal. It was an hour and a half of competitions including one-on-one, two-on-two, five-on-five, and rebounding drills, and it all dealt with identifying ourselves with toughness. That day changed our season around. I was in so much pain the night before in the Lake Superior State game, and practicing that hard hurt my knee very badly, but I walked out with my head held high because God was right by my side. I started the next game and we got smacked because we shot poorly, but we had found our identity. The rest of the season was painful to play through, but God was with me every step of the way.

I was proud with my team's effort to go 20–8, and I was proud of myself for helping lead them even though I was not feeling great the whole season.

God stayed with me the whole off-season even after my stem cell procedure. Everything was falling into place because I became the co-president of the Student Athlete Advisory Committee (SAAC), a student-orientation leader, the Oilers Changing Campus Culture student leader, the basketball captain, and a Fellowship of Christian Athletes (FCA) Officer. Emily Molnar, a member of the women's basketball team at UF, asked me if I wanted to help lead FCA. I was blessed to be asked and said yes on the spot. The Fellowship of Christian Athletes brought me closer to God because I had to be a leader in a Christian setting. I was a leader around campus, in the community, on the playing field, and in life. I got to help teach others about Christ, and how He could change their lives. Everything was going to plan; God had led me to this point because of His beautiful guidance.

My faith in Him encouraged me to go on walks to the Findlay Reservoir to watch the sunset, read the Bible, to attend Revive, which was a worship service on campus on Thursday nights, to attend Sunday morning services at Gateway Church, and to attend FCA on Wednesday nights. God had taken over my life in a very powerful way.

December 3, 2016, at Ferris State, I was hit again. With less than thirty seconds to go in overtime in a tie game, I went to the basket and got fouled. I tried to shoot the lay-up, but I had no explosion off the ground, and I went down in pain. I thought it was just another punch I had taken in basketball, but it grew to be way worse. We won that game because Ricardo Smith stepped up to make the game winning free throw in my place.

I sat out the next couple of days and tried to practice the Wednesday before our game; however, as I was jogging after a ball, my knee gave out. I had been having pain all practice and I knew this was it for a while. I called my parents, and they felt badly for me. I saw some doctors in Toledo. My career was on the verge of being over because my patellar tendon had ripped off my kneecap, and I was going to struggle to live a healthy lifestyle.

I went to practice every day, still teaching, coaching, and working hard in the weight room because I had a role on the team whether I was playing or not.

God has told me through prayer to always smile. I thank Him for saving my life, not because I was going down a wrong path, but because He helped my find my path. My path has made an impact on others. You will always make an impact on someone every day, and He taught me to make an impact on others through faith, smiling, kind words, and energy.

Sitting Out During a Crucial Time

Sitting out with an injury is never easy. Sitting out with a repetitive injury is not easy either. Sitting out in general is difficult. But sitting out when the season progresses, the games become more intense, and post-season implications become apparent, is the most difficult. Sitting out during the GLIAC quarterfinal game against Grand Valley State University was evident of that. I wanted to be able to compete with my teammates out on the floor. I remember talking to another injured teammate, Alex White. We discussed how we felt about not being able to play and sitting out of games like this one hurt even more.

We won that game 67–59 in Croy Gymnasium. It was time to play our rival, Ashland University, at the host school, Ferris State University. The night before the semi-final game, I had a friend come over to the hotel to chat. She is an inspiration for putting life into perspective, is a strong believer in Christ, is very knowledgeable about college athletics, and is just a great friend to talk to about anything. We have had numerous FaceTime conversations about helping one another reach our goals, and one thing she helped me with was tithing.

I started to give money to the church on my own for offering.

We talked about giving ten percent of our earnings in a FaceTime conversation. I used to give nothing because money is valuable to a college student. I did not want to give away five to ten dollars to a church when I did not know what it would do with it. I have broken that barrier now because God has given me life, and if I cannot give ten percent, or whatever I have for that Sunday, then I need to re-evaluate my life. God has given me so much, and I hope once I am making more income I can give back even more to the church because Gateway Church has done amazing things in my life by helping me bring my spiritual life to another level. Gateway Church has made me a happier individual, and if I am out of town for the weekend, I always think about being at Gateway because of the amazing inspirations in life the church has given me.

It was game day, which also happened to be my birthday, March 4. I thought we were ready for the challenge of playing Ashland at a neutral site. We had lost a game against them in their arena, but we beat them at ours. This was the rubber match. Ashland came out firing on all cylinders.

We got down 52–29, and I wanted to be very vocal at halftime, but it was hard to say much because I was not playing. I said a couple things along the lines of, "We've got to guard better because the way they are getting their threes off dribble penetration and kick-outs." The locker room was just silent, and I remember counting to myself that ten out of fourteen heads were down. Dropping heads is never the answer in life. The only thing that you see looking down is the ground and maybe your shoes. When you look at eye level, you see facial expressions and learn more about your surroundings. When you look straight up, you look at God. He is the answer, and He can help you through any tough situation. He could have brought us together and comforted us, but no one was looking that high up. We got blasted in the second half as well, and our body language and leadership was embarrassing because we did not look like Findlay basketball players.

After the game, I met with some of my friends on Ashland's team and wished them luck in the championship game that coming Sunday. I also talked to one of their coaches. I was walking out of Wink Arena and he came over and shook my hand and asked how my recovery was going.

We got chatting about life after basketball, and I said my injury had been amazing because it had exposed me to so much more in life. I talked about how being on crutches for five weeks makes you realize that you take walking for granted, and not just in terms of playing basketball; it is much easier to get around in life when you are able to walk. We had a really good conversation. It was another way to spread the Word: I demonstrated how strong someone can be after defeat and a couple knee surgeries.

Wink Arena was the place where I got injured earlier in the season. On the same day, it was post-season play, my birthday, a rivalry game, and the place where I got injured. I do not believe that this was a coincidence, but more of a place that God wanted me to come back to because of the way He has continued to shape my future as a follower of Christ. I was still in a brace, but during a shoot-around that morning I reenacted the play where I got hurt by walking through it all.

Nobody probably realized what I was thinking, but from the day we found out that we were going to play at Ferris State, my injury was the first thing that went through my head.

I was blessed to go back there one more time because I thought it was what God wanted. He made me look at the big picture, and He made sure I received that message.

This was not how I intended my birthday to go, but I got to spend it with my family, friends, teammates, and coaches. We were still given the opportunity to compete in the NCAA Tournament as the sixth seed in the Midwest Region in Louisville, Kentucky, against Southern Indiana.

This message is for the many student athletes all around the world. If you have never been injured for a long period of time or missed a crucial contest, then it may be hard to relate. Put yourself in the mindset of not being able to play the biggest game of the year against your rival opponent. Think about what you might be feeling on the sideline when all you can do is watch and encourage your teammates. You take a different view of the game; you have a thousand thoughts going through your head about what you would do if playing in the game, but you cannot because you are injured.

It is not a great feeling to miss out, but when you get to go and compete again, you will never take for granted being given that opportunity.

Coaches suspend players for breaking team policy, and they decide to sit them out for a game. This suspension teaches them to be respectful and responsible on and off the playing field; therefore, you can showcase your hard work under the lights. When injuries happen and you cannot control them, it may be harder to deal with since you are not in control of the situation.

The one thing I could control, however, was the moment I was in. I was not sure if I would experience an NCAA Tournament run again. I needed to love the moment and love the success my team and school was having even though I was not playing. I was still on the team, and my role was helping my teammates in intense situations or helping them with a play or action we were running. I gave advice on what I saw so we could succeed as a team. The run in the tournament was different than I thought it would be, but I was on God's team and Findlay's team. My own personal team was pushed aside for the love of my God and teammates.

Your Shadow Is Like a Follower: Wherever You Go, It Goes

Mentors, leaders, and celebrities play a huge part in our society thanks to the advancement in technology and social media at our fingertips. We tend to like someone because of who we see them to be in a video, pictures, or something they did that made the news. Some of these people are perceived only in the way the media portrays them, but this perception is not who they truly are. We have all heard the phrase "being two-faced": meaning when someone is respectful to some people, but disrespectful around others.

God knows all, and He knows who you truly are. He is around you all the time, even when you think no one is watching you. We all look around when we are supposed to be working on an assignment, a chore, or a rep in a workout. We want to see if our boss, coach, or parent is watching us work hard. God knows if you are cheating yourself or someone for whom you are working.

One thing I learned while I was striving to be a better Christian was to listen to Christian music when working out. Some songs are upbeat, while others have a slower beat. No matter, God puts me in the mood to be great because of hearing the music and listening to the lyrics.

Every time I am struggling to push through a workout, I just think about how Jesus carried the cross and died so I could have eternal life. The least I can do during the workout is make myself better, which will make my teammates better, which will reward our loyal fans in the city of Findlay.

For some people, it is not easy to picture God during the day because we get caught up in our busy lives. But making yourself aware of His presence through work, chores, exercise, or sitting around with family and friends can help you grow as a Christian and can inspire someone else to open the Word of God.

Your shadow goes where you go. Your shadow, in this case, is your follower. You get to lead your shadow wherever you go, which means it follows you to the store, school, work, and bed. Would you follow yourself? Are you two-faced? Are you a role model to other people who you encounter in your daily life? Doing the right thing is never wrong. When you are by yourself and no one is watching, that is the person you truly are. That is the person God knows you to be because He knows all and sees all.

I thought about my shadow when I was on a bike ride one sunny day. My shadow was behind me at the time, and it made me think about how my shadow was a follower. When I switched positions, my shadow was in front of me and I had a whole different perspective. This time the shadow was Christ as the leader, and I was the follower. He will lead me in the right direction if I follow His lead. We sometimes try to predict our future. I am a culprit of this because I try to plan everything out instead of letting things happen. I am very future-oriented because I want to be successful, but I have done all the hard work and now God will lead me to where He wants me to be and not where I want to be.

The next time you are outside, just look down at your shadow to see if you are following God or if your shadow is following you. Do what is right because God knows who you are. You can always change bad habits at any time in your life, so make that commitment, make a greater individual commitment the next day, and so on.

Risk-Taking and Adversity

What is risk-taking? Is it doing something you do not usually do? Is it a risk you only do one time because you know it is not smart? Is it a short-term risk or a long-term risk? Will the risk affect you currently? Will the risk affect you forever if it does not work out? Are you willing to take risks? Are you willing to take smart risks? Think about some of the risks you have taken in the past. Were they good decisions? Think about some of the times you could have taken a risk but chose not to. Was it good not to take the risk? Do you regret not taking that risk? Risk-taking will be around forever, so when do you know how and when you should take certain risks? I had an experience to which some of you may relate, or you may recognize a similar risk that may pop up in the future like the following one. My experience may help you make a decision.

I transferred school districts heading into my eighth-grade year. Transferring was not the easiest thing to do. However, if you are looking for something new, why not go after it and see where it leads? After transferring to the Toledo School District, I was frowned upon often.

Nobody in the Bowling Green area liked the fact that I had switched schools. I lost nearly all my friends, and I got nasty text messages that called me a "traitor." I almost regretted my decision as a result. I realized though, that if these former friends of mine were saying these things, I did not want them to be my friends anyway. Maybe I had gotten away from the bad and stepped into the good. This is exactly what happened to me.

God does the same thing in the sense of trying to bring Himself into your everyday life. At first it is not easy; however, being consistent, being patient, and being loyal to Him will eventually work the right way in the end because that is His intention. Psalms 119:105 states, "Your word is a lamp to my feet and a light to my path." This is one of my favorite Bible verses because God is going to give us His love, which will give us the direction we need. He paves the path for us to follow. God gives us everything we need, and it is our responsibility to get on that path.

Why not take a few risks in life? Why not try to challenge yourself to make yourself a better person inside and out? All of the great businesses, organizations, men, and women took a risk down the road because they needed to know what it felt like to fail.

Failing is also called learning. Failing is when you continue to repeat the same mistakes repeatedly because you refuse to listen. Failing is learning because you learn from mistakes or you learn from other failures. You want to do what is right because it is the best thing for you or for someone else. Failing once is temporary, but learning happens your whole life, so why not learn when you fail?

    Risk-taking and adversity are some things that humans go through every day. Adversity can be as simple as waking up a little late in the morning and still having to make it to school or work on time. Not many people embrace adversity because they usually want people to feel sorry for them. I embrace adversity, and I do not want people to feel sorry for me. I want to go through the pain to show that it is more than doable by the fact that I want to do it. Consider the quote from Nelson Mandela, "Do not judge me by my successes, judge me by how many times I fell down and got back up again." Everyone falls. It just happens whether you slip on ice, step on someone's foot, or fall down the stairs. But everyone gets up differently.

Do you need someone to help you up? Does someone need to see that you are hurting first? Do you need to make a scene so you get attention? Or do you just get up on your own and say, "Yes, that hurt, but I am way bigger than that fall, and I will have to go down harder to know what pain feels like." This attitude sets a great example in sports. Everyone falls in sports. Sometimes it is embarrassing, and sometimes you just take a hard fall because of a play. So, get up and keep going like nothing happened. If a teammate notices how you got up from that fall, they will be inspired to get up when they fall because you set an example. This is who our team is, and it may even rattle an opponent. Make falling a strength, not a weakness. You do not need to be physically tough to get up from a fall, but you have to get up with a purpose to keep on competing.

Something in Nature

As consumers of nature we go through our daily lives with the ability to smell the fresh air and to breathe that air. Have you ever thought about why we have the ability to breathe naturally with no oxygen masks? Genesis 1 and 2 state that God created the world including the trees, birds, rivers, etc. If God did not create these things, what would we have? What would Earth look like? Would there even be an Earth?

Have you ever been on a boat, a nature trail, or just walked outside of your house and wondered "what" and "why"? The "what" in this question is, what would I want to be in nature if I had the choice?

For instance, if I was on a walk along a reservoir or river, my options would be the wind, a rock, the water, a boat, the sun, the moon, clouds, grass, sand, trees, a trash can, etc. Let's say my "what" is the water. My "why" is explaining the reason I want to be the water. I would want to be the water because the water brings people close to one another whether that is family or friends. The water is also an example of a place for comfort for the fish and creatures God created to swim and live in that environment.

The water provides food for humans, fish, and a great scenic place for individuals to get away and run, walk, or bike for a workout.

There is another way to look at your "why." If I chose a trash can, most people would just say it smelled and that it was a place to get rid of nasty or used things. I look at it as if someone is throwing away their bad habits, poor choices, or things that they are getting rid of just because they are bad in their life. So, the trash receptacle can give someone the opportunity to start fresh or with a clean slate.

The "what" is easier to select, but the "why" can be challenging. You can think about your "why" as in literal terms of the use that water or a trash receptacle can bring, or the philosophical version of what people are receiving or giving in the terms of a Christian or critical thinker.

I want you to try when you are out in the nature to think about the life and the world God has given you. Look more into the natural side of things because God created the heavens and the Earth. Maybe you will find that it is hard to just pick one thing for that day, or maybe you will struggle to find your "why."

You may find your "what" to be different than what I listed above because of your location, imagination, or just something I left available for you to talk with God about on your nature walk wherever that may lead.

Faith is the foundation of who you are and what you will want to become. Having a strong foundation in your faith and believing that Jesus dying on the cross for you to live the life you have now is the starting point. He is always going to be there for you and will continue to be there for you even if your relationship with Him begins to fade. Continue to trust and believe, and you will know what your purpose is in your life because God has put us in this world for a reason. Find your reasoning by first having faith.

Love

Taking Opportunities for Granted

We all take opportunities for granted. We can earn an opportunity by working hard to achieve something, but why risk that opportunity for doing something you know is not right? As a matter of fact, why complain about something you have wanted to do your whole life? A great example is college athletes. Some college athletes have thrown away opportunities because of drinking, drugs, grades, or other problematic situations that occur on college campuses. I was reading a John Calipari book called, "Success Is The Only Option: The Art Of Coaching Extreme Talent." He caused me to reflect on a time when some of my teammates were late to the weight room. "A scholarship is like a winning lottery ticket; some of you will make the most of it and take advantage of that ticket, and some of you will just throw it in the trash," I told them. I thought this was a great way to explain it because a full scholarship is something student athletes take advantage of and take for granted.

This attitude bothers me because we consider being a student athlete a job. At least I used to think it was a job, but then I realized that it was a luxury and a dream.

I had always wanted to play college basketball, and I was blessed with that opportunity due to hard work and dedication every day growing up. I thought it was a job being a student athlete because there was so much going on my freshman year. I was independent and on my own for the first time, I was a full-time student and an athlete, and I attended lots of social events, clubs, and campus organizations. There was no time for rest. My day looked like this:

- Wake up at 7:00 a.m.
- Eat breakfast
- Attend classes from 8:00 a.m. to 12:00 p.m.
- Eat lunch from 12:00 p.m. to 1:00 p.m.
- Lift weights at 2:00 p.m.
- Practice basketball from 3:30 p.m. to 5:45 p.m.
- Eat dinner at 6:00 p.m.
- Attend occasional night classes from 6:00 p.m. to 9:00 p.m.
- Do homework, shower, go back to the gym and shoot, or hang out with friends.

The next day I woke up and did it all over again. This schedule used to be a hassle and a grind. A busy schedule still is a grind, but my mindset has changed to a more joyful and live-it-up approach. On some days, athletes will just go through the motions because they do not want to be at lifting or working out because they are tired. This mindset does not make sense to me because we have a great opportunity to better ourselves in all aspects of life. As athletes, we get the opportunity to lift weights, practice, and put in the time, so why not put in one hundred percent of our effort and make the most of it? If you are going to be in there, why not make yourself a better player? This translates into the real world because if you don't put forth a full effort for a company you are working for then you will not be meeting company expectations and it will show. If you work hard every day, the results may lead to a raise in salary or a higher position because of your hard work and positive results.

Some people with nice jobs complain about their jobs all the time. They want others to feel sympathy for their hard work. If that is your case, then you are working in the wrong industry. Yes, a job can be hard at times, but it should never be dreadful.

Challenges should be fun and exciting because every day you have a chance to make a difference for the company. In the student-athlete world, when another teammate or a player complains about a certain workout or having to go to practice, it bothers me because it adds negativity to the room. It is just noise that is unnecessary for other players to hear because then it shuts them off and creates a domino effect, which results in a poor practice. If you do not like what you are doing, then why sign on the line on signing day? Embrace the opportunity to be a student athlete because not many get the chance to play, and especially on a full ride.

Some student athletes also take their education for granted. They take the attitude that since their education is paid for they don't have to care so much about classes. Right? Wrong. Many companies want to hire student athletes because they understand teamwork, a busy schedule, and how to balance school, athletics, and free time. If student athletes make the most of their academics and athletics, then almost anyone will be willing to hire them because succeeding in both areas is not easy at all.

Someone is paying for your scholarship whether you think that or not.

At Findlay, tuition is around $40,000 per year, which means that the coaches believe I am worth that much to their program on and off the court. I have spent five years at the University of Findlay because of taking a medical redshirt year. In those five years, my education cost $200,000 plus. I get to graduate debt-free, unlike most students who attend college. Why not make the most of your opportunity, so you will not have any regrets down the road?

    Alcohol and drugs are a huge part of the college scene; some students get caught up in it, and some do not. Alcohol is very easy for students to access because everyone on campus knows someone who will purchase it. And, as a student athlete, you usually know a wide array of students because of being on a team. Faculty know who you are, as do others just by you wearing team gear around campus. This means that you reflect your team and university at all times. Underage students and student athletes take risks when going out to a party with friends. It is not bad to go out with the team and socialize, but why drink and put yourself at risk?

    Drinking can put you in a position to let the team down, yourself down, your family down, your school down, and, depending on how you get in trouble, it can ruin your future.

One night is not worth all of this. I have heard about and seen things like this happen in my collegiate career, and it is just not worth it. No drink of alcohol or drug is worth the risk of your future or eligibility with the team. As a student athlete, we are given so many great opportunities that many students do not receive, and we are more accountable than other students because we are on our team. I reflect the Findlay basketball team, but the example I set is not just for my team; it is for everyone around campus because they will notice my actions. I want my actions to be a positive reflection of my university, team, and myself.

Would I Want to Work with Me?

Working with people can be very difficult and sometimes very frustrating. There are so many different types of people with whom to work: you have the lazy, rude, untrustworthy, hardworking, work-is-the-only-thing-they-care-about, and the does-not-care-about-anybody-else types of people. Yes, there are many other types of employees, but this is just to name a few. If someone had one word to describe you in the workplace and they knew you were not around, what would that word be? Do you think it would be positive? It is a great question to ask behind closed doors. If you had the opportunity to receive these answers after asking a hundred people, do you think you would be disappointed? Would you shut down if they were negative? Or would you do something about it by working on the negative responses you received and making them a strength to make it a more enjoyable workplace for everyone?

I have not been in the workplace before to know what my feedback would be. But I think if you asked yourself this question every day, you would become a better employee.

In coaching, this type of question can be very unusual because other coaches on the coaching staff may have a different response than the players would. Coaches on coaches' evaluations may discuss dedication, effort, listening skills, willingness to meet in early hours, doing the little things, etc. A player would look at the coach from a different perspective. A player will look at it from how a coach is teaching a player or how the coach is to be around off the court. Does the coach have a sense of humor off the court? Is there a balance between being serious when it is time to be serious, and maybe being easy to talk to off the court?

    Just like in the business world, if you are the boss, your employees will have one way to describe you, but the customer may describe you totally differently. Athletics can teach us many things about the business world and life just by the way people can look at one another whether you know that person well or not.

    If you are hesitant about whether you would want to work with yourself then you have some things you need to change. Make a list of the things you like about yourself if you are working for a company.

This may require being a hard worker, willing to work past hours to get tasks completed, or efficient in a certain software. Then list some reasons why you may not want to work for yourself. This could be a lack of motivation, talks behind another employee's back, or thinks that they are always right.

The Strongest Relationship

There are many relationships that are developed in a day, week, month, year, years, and lifetimes. Many relationships last for a short period of time, and some last for a much longer period, but do any relationships last forever? Friends who I had in elementary school are not the same friends I have today. I have two friends who I stay in touch with frequently from that grade level. Junior high was different for me because I transferred to a different school system. I went from a Bowling Green public-school system to St. John's Jesuit Academy, a private-school system in Toledo. The relationships I made at St. John's have lasted longer because I was older and spent a number of years there.

You will continue to form relationships with people in college: teammates, friends, classmates, coaches, and faculty members at the university. College is great because you meet classmates who have the same major, are in the same clubs, and live in the same dorm. These relationships will more than likely last longer than any other relationship in your life because this is the time when you find out who you are through trial and error. You will make mistakes, but it is all about how you deal with those mistakes.

Will you continue to make them, or will you learn from your mistakes and find out who you are and what is important to you? In the work force, you will meet great people and form relationships. Down the road, you may have a wife or husband and kids, and you will have a strong relationship with them. Family and close friends are very strong relationships to have on Earth. But what if you are on a business trip and you are out of town? Who is there for you to be with and talk to? What if you want some time alone or want to share something with someone, but you do not want anyone to say anything? Who do you tell? You may have a secret, great news, or be in the darkest part of your life. Do you have an outlet? What if no one close to you is left on Earth? Do you just keep it in or do you let it out? This is where you find your strongest relationship, and that is between yourself and God. In Mark 2, Jesus heals a paralytic man. People all around believe this man is broken from the outside, but he is more broken on the inside. In Mark 2:5 states, when Jesus saw their faith, he said to the paralytic, "son your sins are forgiven." You are not an accident, but you are significant and special because that is how we are all made.

College has made me realize that the friendships I have built will last a short or long time, but there is one relationship that will last forever from the day I was born until the day I die. Building my relationship with God will have its ups and downs just like any relationship. You will ask God, why? You will think you are doing all the right things, yet somehow the things you care about the most do not work out to your plan. It is not easy to deal with failure because it can be very emotional. Emotions play a major role in life. God can help weather that storm just through prayer, the church, Bible studies, other believers, and opening the Word of God. It is amazing what He can do. He has made me a strong believer even though my relationship with Him can still get stronger. I have surrounded myself with other believers, opened the Word of God, gone to other Bible studies, and prayed. There are other ways to develop a stronger relationship with God, but these are the ways that have helped me.

I have a close family and close friends, but that does not mean I do not have bad moments throughout the day. God is there when I need to talk. And sometimes opening up the Bible and reading a scripture will be exactly what I need to hear.

We have goals and aspirations, but God has the ultimate plan. He has made some of the rough patches in my life happen because He wants to make me stronger and to find out who He wants me to be. I have accepted that and have embraced it with open arms. It took a second injury for me to realize it, but I am glad I have. Findlay has helped me become a stronger person, more faithful, more educated, and a leader. Findlay will always have a special spot in my heart for these things. I have gone to the best high school and college imaginable for me. I know that God helped me make my decisions, and He put me in this position to have a successful career and life. No matter what happens in my life, good or bad, God will be my strongest relationship. He made me. I have a strong relationship with Him, and I know we will continue to grow closer.

Develop relationships with people who can challenge you mentally, physically, emotionally, and spiritually. Having relationships with these types of people will ultimately make you a better person and even a better friend.

You may not think of it that way, but by being around a group of friends who are not motivated, have no discipline, and no love for God is essentially putting yourself in position to be just like them. Over time it will happen even though you may think it is hard to believe. They will get you to talk a certain way, believe a certain thing, and wrap you into a lifestyle that is not meant for the way God has led you to live. Proverbs 17:17 states, "A friend loves at all times, and a brother is born for a time of adversity." John 15:13 says, "Greater love has no one than this: to lay down one's life for one's friends." Think about these Bible verses, and ask yourself these questions: Do I love my friends always? Do I still love and respect my enemies? Do I give thanks for the people who are in my life? Do I pray daily about the ups and downs that the Lord has challenged me with? Grow in a relationship with the people around you by having a Christ-centered focus.

Judging

We look at the world as if we are a big part of many individual lives. As consumers of the world, we try to be involved in people's lives whether it is our business or not. Consumers want to know everything and want to have everything even if it brings no value to themselves personally, but it takes away added value to someone else. Consumers are also advice givers even when they do not abide by their own advice. Trying to tell someone what to do, what they should do, and tell them what they are doing wrong. We are just being hypocritical. We get involved in their dating issues, friendship problems, their sins, or we just want to give advice, whether you actually believe that or not. We are all great advice givers, but we are not all great listeners. We may hear our friend tell us about an issue going on, but before they finish their story, we have already jumped to conclusions because we think we know it all.

Here are some steps to be a great friend and for giving advice:

1. Listen with an Open Mind

    - Let someone explain, tell, and finish their story before thinking/talking about the advice you are willing to give.

2. Ask Questions

    - Do not be afraid to get your questions clarified if there is confusion when helping someone else. This could change your opinions, thoughts, or advice.

3. Think

    - If you just think and talk at the same time, you may contradict yourself, change your mind, come across the wrong way, or hurt someone's feelings.

4. Talk

    - Give your opinion, but still give them the option of making their own decision at the end. No answer is the only option. Let them decide on their own, but just guide that individual along the way.

5. Advice
    - Giving examples and explaining your solutions or advice is key because they may want reassurance or facts.
6. Love
    - Whatever they decide, make sure they know you still love them and you are always willing to talk to them about anything that is on their mind.

Many people need help because they are afraid to be judged by their peers by something they did or that a loved one did to them. As a society, we are so quick to judge someone because of a mistake they have made or them doing something not very intelligent. We have all made mistakes, sometimes even similar mistakes to the ones to which we are making fun.

For example, if someone went into a gas station and stole a candy bar, we may say, "Why would you ever do that?" That is not smart of you, and the Bible says thou shall not steal.
But we may take our colleague's headphones to use without asking permission first. Both are stealing. In both situations something was taken without permission. The headphones can be returned, but what if you damaged them?

This can affect a relationship with someone you respect even though you did not intend to hurt that person.

Unknown Future

When you are blessed to wake up in the morning, what is your plan? What is your goal? What do you want to get accomplished? Do you wake up already having an idea of what you want to do with your day? Or do you just wake up and then think about what you might do? We all wake up differently in the morning. If you wake up with a plan or goal in mind, you are more likely to succeed that day because you will feel like the day was not productive if you do not accomplish those goals. By having a plan, you will likely succeed not only on that day but also later down the road because of the sacrifices and the mindset you had going into every day. There is no guarantee that success will happen, but the chances are more likely in your favor.

I wake up with a plan or a list of things I need to do every day, whether it is getting ready for a school day, preparing for a basketball workout, participating in a lifting session, or catching up on some things I need to do. I went through a big obstacle heading into my redshirt senior season.

It was still unknown how I would be able to perform after my knee surgery in January because the surgery was not guaranteed, and neither was my health playing collegiate basketball the next year. I had major knee surgery in January of 2017 at the Cleveland Clinic and it turned out to be a great decision, after other doctors said I should not ever consider playing basketball again. I had to go through my fourth off-season doing rehabilitation on my knee.

I was in pain throughout the late part of winter and all of spring and summer. I remember thinking to myself, why should I work hard if I am not going to play again? Why should I put in all the time and effort if there is only a fifty-fifty chance I can play? The reason why the injury happened to begin with was because I played basketball and trained really hard. But I committed to work hard every single day because if I was blessed enough to play again then I wanted to be at my best. I wanted to play one more season, and if I was going to play one more season, I was going to train like it was going to be my best season yet.

It is easy not to train hard when you are healthy because you can get into shape easily, play five-on-five with buddies to get reps in, and go to the weight room when you desire, all because you know you get to play the next season.

I had an unknown future, but I wanted to make it a known future because if I was not able to play, I could at least say that I gave it my all to play again. Knowing that I never gave up is a win not just for now, but I know with God's grace that it will be a win from now until my time on Earth has passed.

Coach Ernst was a huge inspiration of mine. Whether I was able to play my 5th year or not, he wanted me to be a part of the team. He preferred that I would be able to play on the court. However, if I was not able to play, then he wanted me to help as if I was a coach on the sidelines.

If you ever get put in a situation to work hard, whether it be applying for a job and going through an interview process or another situation, always wake up with a plan and set goals for the day because this strategy can help your future by being consistent with the decisions you make in the present. It also can change your mindset to keep going in the tough times even though it is always easier to take the easy route at the time. But it is harder to live with the consequences later down the road by not planning and sticking to your goal every single day. Live life with no regrets by making the best decision today.

What Is Giving Back?

Time is the most important thing someone can give throughout their life. It is easy to write a check, donate a gift, or write a letter, but giving up your time for someone else is priceless. Yes, writing a check or a letter and donating a gift are all very nice gestures; however, giving your time to help with an event is even more valuable. Not everyone has money or a gift to donate, but all humans have time. It is what you do with that time that can change or make an impact on one's life. There may be an event in town with which you have no connection and you decide to volunteer and help for three hours on a weekend for a great cause. Volunteers are always needed; non-profit organizations function mainly because of volunteers, so why not help someone? Make time, even when it isn't convenient, to help others. Once you start giving back with your time, you will not want to stop. You will have made connections and relationships with other volunteers and the people the events are helping.

Giving back to the church is something that I never took pride in, but I was guided to a lesson in the Bible about tithing.

I knew that we were supposed to give back to the church, but why? How much? What if I did not have a job? Did I still give? I had a conversation with a long-distance friend of mine. She is a strong Christian who was born in Christian home. She told me about James 1:5, which says, "If any of you lacks wisdom, let him ask God, who gives generously to all without reproach, and it will be given him." We talked about how we are supposed to give ten percent of our earnings to the church. However, we concluded that whatever amount you give is enough for the church. This gift to the church can give someone else the opportunity to grow in their faith because they may need the money more than I do.

 Ever since my friend and I had that conversation, I have given to the church every Sunday. I do not have a job, but my relationship with God is priceless. The money I do have I will give to the church. The church and God have given me new life and a new sense of happiness and comfort.

 My friend helped me create a vision for myself giving to the church: I help the congregation, make mission trips possible, and shape people to Christ who then spread the Word to one another.

One conversation with someone who has the love and a heart for Jesus changed my outlook on tithing and my ways of giving back to the church.

It can be difficult to give back to your high school, college, or non-profit organization because the first time is always the hardest. It can be difficult because you have to break out of your shell to talk to someone you do not know, or you have to talk to someone you have not talked to in a long time. After the first conversation or day of volunteering, it becomes comfortable and uplifting. Maybe asking a friend to give back with you would make it easier. It is similar with walking in your faith for the first time. It is almost impossible to walk in your faith alone. But if you have a friend by your side, it is much easier to walk in your faith because you can hold one another accountable in following God. The Bible talks about serving others but also being served. In 1 Peter 4:10 it states, "Each one should use whatever gift he has received to serve others, faithfully administering God's grace in its various forms." We must be willing to give our time to someone or something else, but in return, if someone wants to do a good deed or a favor for us, we must be willing to be served so they can serve us.

Giving back your time is the most valuable service you can provide. You get the face-to- face interaction, which is life-changing for some of the less-fortunate individuals or those individuals who are battling a disease that is changing their life. So, with their life being changed negatively, why not make a positive impact on them by giving them hope and inspiring them not to give up? What would you want if you were in their shoes? You would want love and attention as well as the knowledge that you matter. You would want to know that you can still make a difference in the world no matter what you are battling.

Jesus gave back in ways that are not humanly possible for us to do. He performed so many miracles. One of His greatest miracles was when He fed five thousand people. Jesus took the only food the disciples had and blessed the five loaves of bread and two fish. He fed the remaining portions to five thousand people. Matthew 14:13-21 says, "When Jesus heard what had happened, he withdrew by boat privately to a solitary place. Hearing of this the crowds followed him on foot from the towns. When Jesus landed and saw a large crowd, he had compassion on them and healed their sick.

As evening approached, the disciples came to him and said, 'This is a remote place, and it's already getting late. Send the crowds away, so they can go to the villages and buy themselves some food. Jesus replied, 'They do not need to go away. You give them something to eat.' 'We have here only five loaves of bread and two fish,' they answered. 'Bring them here to me,' he said. And he directed the people to sit down on the grass. Taking the five loaves and the two fish and looking up to Heaven, he gave thanks and broke the loaves. Then he gave them to the disciples, and the disciples gave them to the people. They all ate and were satisfied, and the disciples picked up twelve basketfuls of broken pieces that were left over. The number of those who ate was about five thousand men, besides women and children."

This story shows that Jesus was about giving and making every person feel important and equal. The normal person would not have done what He did in this situation. They would have crumbled, gave up, said it was impossible, or would have given an excuse.

Jesus did all of this with love. He is caring and is the almighty Lord and Savior. He found a way to make the impossible the possible.

We are born to be followers of Jesus; however, we need to be leaders in worship. We can all be leaders just by spreading the Gospel. He gave the effort and time to others and that is what we can do in our lives. We can make a difference by giving to others who are less fortunate. Doing gracious acts of kindness is a way to show Jesus shining through you and around you.

So why not give more? We all have extra time in our busy schedule to help and make an impact on others. Why not give just a little more than what you are giving now? Think about if everyone on your team, business, school, or whatever you care deeply about gave just a little bit more than they are currently giving. How much more would get done? Think how much better the results would be. It works the same way in giving back, and one of the ways Jesus made an impact on other people was performing miracles such as feeding five thousand people.

Inward and Outward

Pastor Matt is the pastor at the University of Findlay. He has given me so much advice and knows all his students very well. He discussed the incoming freshmen students' first day of class in one of his sermons. He mentioned that all the students were worried about what they would wear. Students think that their outward appearance will determine whether they will be well liked, be noticed on campus, or whether they fit in with all the students.

He compared this worry about appearances to a book. The outside cover may be bland and not have much color or fancy writing, but you would miss what was inside of it if you never opened the book. That comparison was apt for high school students, college students, what to wear for interviews, and what to wear to your professional job. The outside is important, but if you want to make a good impression, know what is on the inside and show that to others.

Get to know as many people as possible. Friends are something you cannot have enough of in your life.

They can help you through the difficult times, you can make each other smile just by walking by, and you may be able to help one another down the road in your career paths. The bond of friendship will last forever if you choose to make it last.

The decisions you make and the people you associate yourself with shape who you are. Make the right decisions first by surrounding yourself with the people who can make you a better person and who can help you strive for greatness. Surrounding yourself with these people will ultimately allow them to become your closest friends. I am not saying to block out all the people who do you wrong; it may help them to be mentored by you. Everything you say or do to them can be an influence in changing their inward appearance. They are already being perceived one way by their outward appearance; therefore, changing their inward appearance can, in fact, change their outward appearance to others. What will you do today, a week from now, a month from now, or a year from now to help your inward growth? Will this affect your outward appearance?

Will it make an impact on both your inward and your outward appearance?

What are the daily steps that are you willing to do to change your inward appearance or to take that next step in growing toward the person God wants you to become?

God wants us to love our brothers and sisters. We should not hate anyone but love everyone. Imagine the world full of love. The many types of love are broken down into loving God, others, and yourself. Love these three as you would want to be loved by someone else.

The world would be full of Christians that love one another. There would be less unhappy people, strong and confident individuals, no crime, and so many joyful people that cannot wait to spread the Word of God in a loving and caring way that is unbreakable.

Motivation

Vision

We all see the world differently. But no matter how we see the world, we all have a vision. We have a vision about how high school is going to go, how college is going to go, what our first job will be, how much money we will make, where we will live, and the adventures we want to take in life. All our visions are positive outlooks. We all have plans for how our day and night should go.

Take prom, for example. If you ever went to a prom, you probably remember how you wanted the night to go. In your mind, it most likely consisted of a romantic dinner, picture-perfect weather, fun at the dance, and an after-prom party full of laughter and joy. Did the night go exactly as you envisioned? Probably not. Something might have gone wrong or the night took an unexpected turn.

Not everything is controllable. But what you can control is your vision and your outlook every day for the rest of your life. What is your vision? What do you want to get accomplished in the day? What do you want to get accomplished in your life?

If what you are doing today does not lead to your long-term vision, then the day is wasted. If you are not taking steps in the right direction toward that vision, then you do not care enough about your vision. Some people want their vision and dream to just happen, but you control it and you must make it happen. Things just do not happen by accident. They happen by having strong faith and believing in the creator.

What is your vision? Whatever that vision is, write it down. Look at it every single day and go out in the world and execute that vision.

UTC Boston 2017

God changes your life in many ways if you believe in Him. Some people believe that things happen for a reason. I think things do happen for a reason and the reason is that God wants them to happen. He puts obstacles in our lives to test our strength in Him. Some live up to the challenge, some give up, and some just let things happen.

I was notified about a trip 3-4 months prior to the actual date of the training camp of starting in June at a typical Fellowship of Christian Athletes meeting on Wednesday night. It was the Ultimate Training Camp in Boston, Massachusetts. This camp was sponsored by Athletes in Action. Its purpose was to help student athletes and professional athletes apply the Gospel to sport, experience it through sport, and make it the language of sport. Many athletes can only relate to sports because it dominated our lives at the collegiate level. God helped develop our skills and abilities, and we may thank God for them. But what is our mindset in competition? Mindset is a challenge for most athletes. I thought UTC would be a great experience for me and other student athletes at Findlay.

God was telling me to try something new, to make a difference in others' lives, and to help me to continue to grow closer to Him through my sport. I was dedicated to making this trip happen. I invited all the FCA attendees and many wanted to go, but when the time came, only four attended the amazing trip.

Taylor Bolinger (track and field/cross country), Hailey Bryan (softball), Tre Wells (wrestling), and I.

We all have different stories and we are all from different locations, but we all wanted to grow stronger in our faith. We took the twelve-hour trip in my 2010 Ford Escape. We learned a lot about one another. We discussed family, friends, music, academics, and the experience ahead of us. Jack Ridge, who helps fund for many of the ministries on the Findlay campus also helped fund this trip. My relatives also helped make this trip possible such as Grandma Gardner, the Hammer family, my Uncle Mike, the Rutherford family, and my Uncle Gary. They were very generous and kind, and I cannot thank them enough for helping me out.

There was a risk because no one from Findlay had ever attended one of these AIA ultimate training camps events before. After the first evening with my roommates and other student athletes, I found myself happier and more mindful of God, and that was because I was with other athletes growing with God in my life and sport. The first thing I learned was what "Audience of One" means. God alone is worthy of our worship.

As student athletes at the collegiate level, we often got caught up trying to please our coaches, parents, fans, teammates, and ourselves. I idolized certain players, but now I look at them as role models. An idol is anything that begins to function as a substitute for God in your life. This can consume your heart and your time. I have role models in my life, but God is who I look to every day for guidance.

We had the opportunity to display what Audience of One means by competing in a volleyball game. Audience of One means that we play for God. The question we need to ask ourselves is, do our idols love us back? Our idol may not even know we exist. The answer is that God loves us no matter what. If we worship Him and practice having Him in competition, then our attitude, effort, and interactions during competitions will be better, and in return, will help us play better.

Audience of One was the first principle we learned. The fourth principle we learned, and the one I could relate to the most, was called "Hurtin' for Certain." This principle made me think more about Satan. Satan has limited power, but his influence is very high. Satan can punish us and put us down the wrong path by making bad choices. The mission of Satan is to steal, kill, and destroy. He is not an excuse for poor decisions.

Isaiah 55: 8-9 talks about how God promises to bring us good in every circumstance. God knows what He is doing even though we do not, and God does not always allow us to understand why we suffer in some situations. He will not tell us how life will work out.

The way I was hurtin' was through my injuries. My mindset had changed to find the good in being injured and having a couple of knee surgeries. The injuries have brought me closer to God and put my life into perspective. I am blessed to have the little things in life. If you take sports out of my life, I can still make an impact on others. Ultimately, God redeems suffering for our good and His glory. We need to ask God's spirit to enable us to deal with suffering in a way that we can honor and glorify Him in every way possible.

In sports, we deal with tough times, trials, and challenges such as other teammates' attitudes, coaches' criticism of our performance, arguing with officials, keeping our ultimate goal on our mind, halftime interactions with teammates when things are not going well, and making a good impression on fans by performing at a high level. God challenges us with small obstacles and enormous tasks whether it be for a day, month, year, or lifetime.

It is all about whether we embrace the challenges even though it may be hard at first. But staying true to Him will lead you to Heaven and happiness. Psalms 62:1 states that "my soul finds rest in God alone." This means that if we believe in Him we will find peace in life.

Advice to Younger Self

Is life one big, exciting adventure, or is it many lives broken up into one person's experience? Some would say it is one big journey, and others would say it is many chapters to one book. There is an argument for both sides.

Some people go through life not regretting a single thing they have done because they believe everything happens for a reason. Others might say that they want to forget some of the mistakes or memories from their life. Some adults in their forties and fifties have a stable job, kids, and a home, and they continue to support their children in every way possible. Do these parents look back and say, "I wish I would have done this as a kid, or this in high school, or this in college?" The answer is yes, most of them do. Parents relive the things they wish they could have done differently if they were younger. However, maybe their child does not want to live the same way as their parent did, whether that is doing a certain hobby, focusing on a certain major, or playing a certain sport. Every child is different; they want to live the way God intends them to and how they personally want to live their life.

Retirement is a great way to reflect on your life, whether it was the challenges you overcame or the things you wish you would have done differently.

I want to be able to live my life and have no regrets. I want to say I did it God's way by following his guidance. Song of Solomon 2:12 says that God is good. It is easy to say that God is good when things are going well, but how about when they are not going the way that you intended? God is still good no matter what our challenges are or the difficult times we go through. I believe we should never ignore our pasts by saying that something did not happen because all the great inventors, actors, athletes, and business owners made mistakes in order to succeed. Thomas Edison had many failures trying to invent the light bulb, but eventually he got it to work because he persevered and never gave up on himself. Learning from the past is hard for our society to do because it shows that we erred. No one wants to be wrong or to admit they are wrong but owning up to their faults could save their career and change their life in a positive way.

What advice would you give to your younger self? Where would you start?

I am not talking about the time you got a seventy percent on a final exam. Maybe, instead, it is the way you approached that final exam. Perhaps you deserved to receive that exam score of a seventy because of the effort you put forth. But usually an exam will not affect your life too drastically unless a seventy percent is your average score in every class you have taken. I am talking about the people you have met along the way, including the group you decided to be with, organizations you did not join but wish you did, or, the biggest one, not committing yourself to God as soon as you could, so you could have been saved for life on Earth and the life that is to come.

There is some advice I would give to my younger self: I only knew one way to compete and that was 100%. I believed winning in anything I did was the most important thing. Looking back I should have served more in high school to make a greater impact in Toledo. I wish I would have had God by my side during the tough decisions I had to make on where to go to college and what I wanted to get accomplished in my time at Findlay.

However, I would not change my path for anything because even through the rough times, I have learned what to do and what not to do. It was hard for me to admit that I made some wrong decisions, but after I admitted them I realized it was easier to live with my mistakes because they ultimately made me a better person.

Back to the first question at the beginning of this chapter: Is life one big, exciting adventure or is it many lives broken up into one person's experience? It is one big adventure with many different steps along the way. Your life is a never-ending book; it will continue forever with new chapters being written daily. Therefore, live life every day with Christ shining through you and around you, and you will never regret a day in your life. Matthew 5:13-16 says, "You are the salt of the earth. But if the salt loses its saltiness, how can it be made salty again? It is no longer good for anything, except to be thrown out and trampled by men. You are the light of the world. A city on a hill cannot be hidden. Neither do people light a lamp and put it under a bowl. Instead they put it on its stand, and it gives light to everyone in the house. In the same way, let your light shine before men, that they may see your good deeds and praise your Father in heaven."

Relationship Building

People are everywhere, so why not develop the best relationship possible with them? Coaches talk about how you only get one chance to make a first impression. It is very simple to say and very easy to do. Think about that. Think about it from the view that each encounter could be your first or last impression on someone, so why not be the best you can be all the time?

Smiling is just like yawning; both are contagious. Yawning means your brain needs oxygen (in other words, you're fatigued). Smiling means you can bring joy, not just to yourself, but to others as well. If I am walking downtown and I see someone smiling, that brings me joy. No matter how tough life is, why not smile? Why not make an impact on somebody, whether you know them or not? Why not make a difference in the world just by smiling?

Taren Sullivan, a member of the UF men's basketball team, has made tough times easier on me because he is always smiling. He may have had a bad game, but that does not affect the next day for him because he has moved on and he is smiling.

He does not want to bring others down, which is a credit to the kind of person he is. If I am having a good or bad day, and I see him at practice or on campus, he is always smiling and dancing and that makes me happy. These are the type of friends you want to surround yourself with because these people are comforting, relatable, caring, and fun to be around because they love others and do not bring anyone down with them on bad days.

There are some people who just do not like people. They say things like "I hate that person," or "I do not like that person," or "That person is always rude to me." Do you ever wonder why they are mean, rude, or treat others poorly? They most likely do not smile, do not have a balanced lifestyle, or they do not have faith. Life is too short not to laugh and smile. I am not saying there are never bad days because there are; however, do not show your struggle in front of other people because then they will be down and have a bad day too. Make an impact on others with a smile instead of poor body language. By the end of the day, if you are lying in bed or need to talk to your best friend and cry, then do it because it is healthier that way.

Do not bring hundreds of people down because of one bad day; just keep smiling and the hard times will not even seem so hard anymore.

Being a college athlete is challenging at times. You are always on a time schedule. An average day may consist of a team breakfast at 7:30 a.m., followed by classes from 8:00–12:30 p.m., then lunch, then lifting at 2:00 p.m., followed by practice, dinner, and homework and studying in the evening. This schedule prepares you for the real world.

My first two-and-half years at Findlay, I was just a student athlete. Why not try to be more? College usually only comes around one time, and it prepares you for being a mature adult, while setting you up for your future. I realized that I went to Findlay to play basketball, but with a free education, why not get the most out of it in all aspects? I have gotten more involved on campus with the Fellowship of Christian Athletes, Student Athlete Advisory Committee, Oilers Changing Campus Culture, orientation leader, helping with the Special Olympics basketball teams, and anything that is asked of me to do in the community. I want to meet as many people as possible, and build great relationships with students, faculty, and the community.

Yes, my schedule is crazy; however, why not be busy and do something productive with people like myself who are trying to make a difference? I enjoy helping others, and maybe I go overboard doing it, but I would not want to change my experience for anything. I am not saying that this way of life is for all student athletes, but if you want to make a difference then start out by helping a club or organization on campus. If you think you can handle more, then do so because you will continue to meet new students and faculty with whom you will be in contact the rest of your life.

Be Ready for the Unexpected

Many crazy things, good and bad, happen in life. Usually we do not understand why they happen. When someone gets injured, a backup or role player needs to be ready. You never know when injuries or suspensions may happen. Or perhaps that starter is just not playing well, and the team needs someone who is willing to step up. Always stay ready because you never know when that opportunity will happen. It may not necessarily be when someone gets hurt or goes down; maybe the coach just wants to make a substitution to prove a point. If you are a scout team player, always stay ready because you never get a second chance to make a first impression when getting to play in the game for the first time of your career. One of my graduate assistant coaches from Findlay, Caleb Williams, was a full-time assistant for one year, and after that season he became the Head Men's Basketball Coach at University of Northwestern Ohio.

He is a great example of a great leader on and off the court. He is very positive, a great Christian, and a great coach. He wanted this opportunity to happen, but he just did not realize that it would come so soon.

He was ready though, because of all the hard work he put in during college, as a graduate coach, and as an assistant coach, and that is why he received this great opportunity at a young age.

After six games in the 2016–17 season, I got hurt again. Trey Smith, who had decided to redshirt, had to come off the bench because I was out for the rest of the season. He instantly made a great impact. He always stayed ready, and he had a great mindset for competing with the team for the rest of the season. Obviously, I was devastated about not being able to play, but Ephesians 6:11 states, "Put on the full armor of God so that you can fight against the devil's evil tricks." I have put on my armor of God; therefore, my teammates and coaches can see the happiness and love through me seeing God. There is evil that strikes but overcoming that evil by protecting yourself with God is the best shield you can possibly have even in the hardest and most sudden moments.

Be ready, stay humble, and be excited for when great opportunities happen so you can make the most of them. Luke 21:36 says, "Be alert at all times. Pray so that you have the power to escape everything that is about to happen and to stand in front of the Son of Man."

Praying can go a long way but wondering if God is hearing your prayer is sometimes difficult. You cannot always talk to other friends about situations you are going through because you may not want anyone to know. God understands what you are going through in your life, and He is always listening to you. Taking deep breaths in prayer and letting you breathe in God's love is something that is unconditional and unexplainable when you have that relationship with Him.

Monday Treatment

Not many people like to wake up on a Monday because it is the first day of the week. A Monday means grumpy individuals at work: you are fatigued, feel lazy, and are already looking forward to Friday. We all dislike Mondays because they are the first day of the week. Well, Monday is not the first day of the week, so there is no reason to hate it anymore! Not everyone works Monday to Friday, but most do because that is what their job entails.

Sunday is the first day of the week, and since we all love Sundays because they are still part of the weekend, then why not treat them that way? Worshiping on Sunday is the right way to start off your week. You get to hear the Gospel, interact with people who want to be in church, sing to great music, and make a greater commitment to God. I can guarantee that your Monday will be more enjoyable if you take the approach that Sunday is the first day of the week and you start it off the right way by worshiping. On Monday you will be energetic, passionate, faithful, loving, and motivated. Your employees are going to want to have some of you sprinkled on them. You can tell them that worshiping on the first day of the week is helpful and beneficial.

Worshiping on Sunday will make work more enjoyable; you will feel like you can conquer any task that is given to you. You will stop looking forward to the weekend, and you will start living in the present. If you start looking at anything in the future, it will be the beginning of the week because encountering God in your weekly routine will make you want more of Him. You will want to learn more about Him, listen to him through music, and read about Him in the Bible. You will own every single day because He can shape your day and week not just once but for an entire lifetime.

Motivation/Inspiration

Every person is motivated differently to do something they desire. If you go to work from 8:00 a.m. to 5:00 p.m., you must be motivated to do it. You cannot just say that you work only to feed your family or to get by living a somewhat-happy lifestyle. If you do not go to work with passion or energy, then who would want to work with you? What is passion? A lot of teachers say you need passion, but what is it? Passion is something you care deeply about; it is the drive inside of you that can potentially create emotion because you want what is best for that special something or someone.

Think about the people who are not motivated to challenge themselves or make others better. Do you like to be around these people? Is it difficult to have in-depth conversations with them? It is hard for me to understand these individuals because I am easily motivated. My biggest challenge is figuring out why some people are not motivated.

How can I motivate them to pursue a career or participate in activities they would like to do for fun? Everything you do is motivating to others. If you go to the gym and work out on the elliptical machine, that is motivating to someone.

People may see you go to the gym or see you working hard on the elliptical and it inspires them to work harder or potentially go to the gym the next day. That person who saw you may tell their friends or roommates about you working out and that may get them excited about going to the gym.

    We all have a chance to make a difference in the world just by being motivating. Motivation goes hand in hand with passion. An example of motivation for me is not needing coffee to wake me up, or an energy drink before I go to class or practice because I am already motivated to make an impact on someone else's life. I am motivated because I want to impress my family and represent them well. I want to make them proud of me. I wear a name on my back and it is their name. My attitude and behavior reflects my family, and I want that reflection to be positive. I also have a philosophy that if I am not tired by the end of the day, then I did not do enough for someone else. I did not use all my passion and energy that day; God gave me a big heart, and I did not use it to my highest potential.

    I am willing to say that I will utilize the mindset and heart that God gave me. He has given me most of what I need but some of it is a skill that must be learned as well.

God gives you what you need and using your gifts is sometimes the hardest part because no one wants to go through the pain or struggle to be the best. Some people want to be the best without going through the process. The process should be fun because the saying "Hard work pays off" should be the case by giving all your effort as a Christian.

Everyone is different, but what makes you different in becoming the best version yourself? We all have role models growing up, whether it is a celebrity, star athlete, parent, grandparent, sibling, etc. We can be motivated and inspired by our role models, but until we go out and do something about making a difference in the world then we are not being a role model to anyone else. We should all look at one another as a role model of Christ. He died on the cross for us, and the least we can do is give something to the world He created.

Role models are supposed to be that person that we as humans can look up to for guidance. I want to be an example of what other kids, young adults, and adults can look up to for guidance or a mentor when they need help.

I was a role model to so many kids in high school but did not realize it until I was almost ready to graduate. Kids looked up to me at camps; I'd have conversations with them, take pictures, and give them high-fives. When I was a kid I looked up to high school players, so I wanted to motivate other kids now that I am in that position. This was especially true when I got to college because I think you can make an even bigger impact at that level.

Credits

I have learned many things along the way about life, academics, faith, and athletics. I have also learned lessons for myself and lessons I can pass on to other people. No one ever gets to where they are today because they did it alone. Some may think they did it alone, but my guess is that someone helped them out with a connection, did them a favor, or helped them learn from their own mistakes or someone else's mistakes. I had all the above. I had great parents, siblings, family members, friendships, coaches, teammates, and other people helping me along the way. I took a path that I never intended, but it was the path I took, and I would not have wanted it any other way. I am proud of who I am and who I will still become.

Growing up, my brother was very competitive, which benefited me because he pushed me to be good whether it was in a sport or while playing a video game. Despite our competitiveness, we still loved each other at the end of the day. We always went back at it the next day because it was fun and it made us both better competitors.

My sister was a little different because no younger brother wanted to play with his older sister. We enjoyed each other's company because she was my outlet for relaxing, not competing. I was thankful for that balance she gave me. She worked many jobs in high school and in college, which shows her initiative. Some are not willing to seek out jobs, but she was.

My dad has always been involved with sports. He encouraged me to go to the gym any day I wanted to starting in about first grade. He was always there for my basketball games and all my other sporting events growing up. He took me to all the AAU games and coached me until I was going into high school. Like any father who is also a coach, he was probably the hardest on me. But his support over the years and his toughness made me tougher mentally and physically, and was a key reason I was able to earn a college basketball scholarship.

My mom gave me my sense of humor, but also challenged me to be my best version of myself. I got my competitive spirit from my dad and brother, and I got my sense of humor from my mom. I got a great balance growing up. My mom was also very supportive about everything I had going on. She is the one person I can talk to about anything because she is a listener and a true believer in me. She is also growing in faith, and I think her willingness to go to church several years ago helped me get to where I am spiritually.

Another family member who helped me along the way and probably does not realize it is my Grandma Gardner. She selflessly took care of seven children in a small household and has always focused on other people, especially family. She is so heartfelt and is very sweet and generous. My Grandpa Gardner was the same way before he passed away. He retrieved my first home-run ball, was there for my first birdie, and taught me to support family at any cost.

My grandma on my mom's side is very outspoken. She will not miss an event of mine for anything. She has supported me through activities, sporting competitions from grade school to college, and will always be that way because she likes watching me do the things I love. She even attended my college games when I was hurt because she loved me and the Findlay community. I will never forget those moments.

These people taught me many different lessons, but if I do not apply these lessons to my life then I have not used my resources or the things they were trying to teach me along the way. I want to be a great husband, father, teacher, grandparent, and role model because that is my calling on this Earth. I want to be the best I can be in all of these roles, so I can make a positive impact on people in the future.

We all need guidance in life, whether from a family member, friend, relative, or mentor. These people can teach us what to do and what not to do from their own experiences. Listening to them may sometimes be difficult because we all think we have this thing called "life" figured out, but no one on Earth does.

Believing in God and having faith is key because not every person has someone they can look to for guidance. Opening the Gospel every single day can bring the guidance we all need because it is the most valuable guidance one can have.

Author Impressions

"I have been coaching college basketball players for the past 26 years. In that time, I've never had the pleasure to coach anyone with as many positive qualities as Austin Gardner. Austin came from a good life, but it's his consistent and motivated approach to always achieve at the highest level that has been remarkable. We all define success differently in life. For me, Austin Gardner will graduate from The University of Findlay this Spring as one of the most successful student-athletes in our program's history. Despite adversity, he has blazed a path of glory on the court, in the classroom, in this city, and in his faith journey that may never be matched."
- Charlie Ernst, Head Men's Basketball Coach, University of Findlay

"Austin Gardner no longer surprises me. He is a most remarkable young man as I have encountered. Grounded in his faith, he embraces life and shares his blessings with others. Using his God-given gifts to his fullest, Austin consistently leads those around him to better themselves as people, to make the most of their talents and to inspire them to excellence in their life's vocations and spiritual journeys."
- Chris Brooks, former Principal of Findlay City Schools (24 years), current Academic Coach, University of Findlay

"No matter how long I am blessed with the role of coach, Austin will always be at the top as I think back to the players I have been able to coach. Austin is a rare breed in that he has the ability to be a fierce competitor while also maintaining a gracious and humble spirit. Austin has used adversity as a platform for growth and has come out better for it; he is a star in the making."
- Caleb Williams, Head Men's Basketball Coach, University of Northwestern Ohio.

"Austin Gardner is a leader. He has led his basketball teams and has led the University of Findlay Fellowship of Christian Athletes with an amazing combination of grace and love. More than anything, he cares about the people around and it is evident in his writing and all he does in life."
- Andy Lynch, President, District VIII of Fellowship of Christian Athletes

"I am delighted to introduce Austin Gardner as an outstanding University of Findlay student-athlete. During this year's basketball season, you could watch him make fantastic plays before a packed house of cheering fans in our famous Croy Gymnasium--flawless lay-ups completed despite repetitive, painful injuries throughout his college years. But Austin's triumphs on the court do not sum him up, not even close. The grit and grace of his faith define him. Austin has a ready smile when things are good and when they are not. He leads and serves tirelessly in many campus organizations, buoyed by belief in the plan that God has for his life--whatever obstacles and opportunities that plan may present. He is a student of all God has to teach him."
- Katherine Fell, President, University of Findlay

Made in the USA
Middletown, DE
19 April 2018